THE ULTIMATE MOTORCYCLING QUIZ BOOK

PHILIP CARTER

THE ULTIMATE MOTORCYCLING QUIZ BOOK EXPLAINED

From Barry Sheene to Valentino Rossi and the Dakar Rally to MotoGP, this quiz book comprises 80 quizzes each containing ten questions to test even the most knowledgeable of biking enthusiast.

If you know which company produces the Roadmaster or the name of the first Superbike World Champion, then this is the book for you.

CONTENTS

SESSION 1: GENERAL (1)   6-15
Quiz 1:   History of the Motorcycle
Quiz 2:   International Motorcycling Federation
Quiz 3:   It's All About the Bike
Quiz 4:   Manufacturers
Quiz 5:   Motorcycling Legends
Quiz 6:   Motorcycling Records
Quiz 7:   Great Rides (1)
Quiz 8:   Great Rides (2)
Quiz 9:   Miscellany (1)
Quiz 10:   Anagrams – Circuits

SESSION 2: TRACK RACING   16-25
Quiz 1:   MotoGP (1)
Quiz 2:   MotoGP (2)
Quiz 3:   MotoGP (3)
Quiz 4:   GP World Championship {Pre-MotoGP} (1)
Quiz 5:   GP World Championship {Pre-MotoGP} (2)
Quiz 6:   World Superbikes (1)
Quiz 7:   World Superbikes (2)
Quiz 8:   Sidecar World Championship
Quiz 9:   British Superbikes (1)
Quiz 10:   British Superbikes (2)

SESSION 3: ROAD RACING   26-35
Quiz 1:   North-West 200 (1)
Quiz 2:   North-West 200 (2)
Quiz 3:   Ulster Grand Prix
Quiz 4:   Macau Motorcycle Grand Prix
Quiz 5:   Manx Grand Prix (1)
Quiz 6:   Manx Grand Prix (2)
Quiz 7:   Classic TT (2013-2019)
Quiz 8:   Southern 100 Road Races

| Quiz 9: | Scarborough |
| Quiz 10: | Other Irish Road Races |

SESSION 4: ISLE OF MAN TT (1) 36-45
Quiz 1:	Isle of Man TT - General (1)
Quiz 2:	Isle of Man TT: 1907-1914
Quiz 3:	Isle of Man TT: 1920s
Quiz 4:	Isle of Man TT: 1930s
Quiz 5:	Isle of Man TT: 1945-1959 (1)
Quiz 6:	Isle of Man TT: 1945-1959 (2)
Quiz 7:	Isle of Man TT: 1960s (1)
Quiz 8:	Isle of Man TT: 1960s (2)
Quiz 9:	Isle of Man TT: 1970s (1)
Quiz 10:	Isle of Man TT: 1970s (2)

SESSION 5: ISLE OF MAN TT (2) 46-55
Quiz 1:	Isle of Man TT: 1980s (1)
Quiz 2:	Isle of Man TT: 1980s (2)
Quiz 3:	Isle of Man TT: 1990s (1)
Quiz 4:	Isle of Man TT: 1990s (2)
Quiz 5:	Isle of Man TT: 2000s (1)
Quiz 6:	Isle of Man TT: 2000s (2)
Quiz 7:	Isle of Man TT: 2010s (1)
Quiz 8:	Isle of Man TT: 2010s (2)
Quiz 9:	Isle of Man TT: 2022
Quiz 10:	Isle of Man TT - General (2)

SESSION 6: DISCIPLINES AND EVENTS 56-65
Quiz 1:	Enduro (1)
Quiz 2:	Enduro (2)
Quiz 3:	Motocross
Quiz 4:	Speedway
Quiz 5:	Trials
Quiz 6:	Electric Bikes
Quiz 7:	Supermoto

Quiz 8:	Endurance World Championship
Quiz 9:	Dakar Rally
Quiz 10:	Pikes Peak International Hill Climb

SESSION 7: ENTERTAINMENT   66-75

Quiz 1:	At the Movies (1)
Quiz 2:	At the Movies (2)
Quiz 3:	Celebrity Bikers
Quiz 4:	Literature
Quiz 5:	Music (1)
Quiz 6:	Music (2)
Quiz 7:	Television (1)
Quiz 8:	Television (2)
Quiz 9:	Video Games (1)
Quiz 10:	Video Games (2)

SESSION 8: GENERAL (2)   76-86

Quiz 1:	Anagrams – Manufacturers
Quiz 2:	True or False?
Quiz 3:	Circuits (1)
Quiz 4:	Circuits (2)
Quiz 5:	Snaefell Mountain Course (1)
Quiz 6:	Snaefell Mountain Course (2)
Quiz 7:	Who Am I?
Quiz 8:	Miscellany (2)
Quiz 9:	Miscellany (3)
Quiz 10:	Anagrams – Riders

ANSWERS   87-103

SESSION 1: GENERAL (1)

Quiz 1: History of the Motorcycle

1. True or False: The first commercial design for a self-propelled bicycle had three wheels?
2. What were the names of the two men who built the 'Reitwagen,' the first effective two-wheeled vehicle powered by a petrol engine?
3. Alongside the Reitwagen, can you name the two other motorcycles which can lay claim to being the first motorcycle?
4. Which motorcycle, produced between 1894 and 1897, was the first production motorcycle?
5. Which company is the oldest motorcycle manufacturer still in existence?
6. In what year did Royal Enfield introduce their first motorcycle?
7. True or False: During World War I, Triumph Motorcycles sold more than 30000 of its Type H Model to allied forces?
8. Which company was the largest motorcycle manufacturer in the World in 1920?
9. Which company supplied 126000 motorcycles to the British armed forces between 1937 and 1950?
10. In which US State was there a confrontation between bikers and police during a biker rally in 1947?

Quiz 2: International Motorcycling Federation

1. In what year was the International Motorcycling Federation (FIM) founded?
2. In which country would you find the FIM Headquarters?
3. In 1994, FIM became the first international sporting federation to publish what?
4. True or False: Since 2019, helmet manufacturers have been required to submit helmets to FIM for testing?
5. Who became President of FIM in 2018?
6. How many motorcycle racing disciplines are covered by the FIM?
7. True or False: FIM was granted the official status of a Recognised Federation by the International Olympic Committee at the 2012 Olympic Games in London?
8. What does the design of the FIM Headquarters building resemble?
9. Can you name the 15-time FIM World Champion and 10-time Isle of Man TT winner who was appointed as a board member of the International Foundation for Motorcycling, when it was established by FIM in 2020?
10. To the nearest ten, how many national motorcycle federations were represented by FIM in 2022?

Quiz 3: It's All About the Bike

1. True or False: The first front-wheel brakes to appear on bikes were added in 1938 by Norton Motorcycles?
2. Who developed the two-stroke expansion chamber in the 1950s?
3. What system became standard in the late 1980s to improve rider safety?
4. What was the first production motorcycle to use a liquid cooling system?
5. What is the CG150 Titan Max, launched to the Brazilian Market by Honda in March 2009, powered by?
6. Which manufacturer was on the verge of bankruptcy in 1959 when Herbert Quandt acquired a controlling interest in the firm?
7. What was the first production motorcycle to use disc brakes on the front and rear?
8. In which decade did the electric start first become a standard feature on production motorcycles?
9. True or False: In 2016, the European Union reduced emissions permitted from new motorcycles to 0.17 gram of hydrocarbons, 0.09 gram of nitric oxides, and 1.14 grams of carbon monoxide?
10. Which technology was patented by Frederick William Lanchester in 1902?

Quiz 4: Manufacturers

1. True or False: Gilera was purchased by Piaggio in 1969?
2. With which manufacturer did Barry Sheene win consecutive World titles in 1976 and 1977?
3. How many Britten V1000s were produced in total?
4. In which country was the manufacturer OSSA founded?
5. Which manufacturer, founded in 1903, has its headquarters in Milwaukee, Wisconsin, USA?
6. In which decade of the 20th Century was Ducati founded?
7. Ferdinando Innocenti was the founder and creator of which motorcycle?
8. Which manufacturer produces the Roadmaster bike?
9. In which country would you find the headquarters of Husqvarna?
10. Can you name the oldest global motorcycle brand in continuous production?

Quiz 5: Motorcycling Legends

1. Which MotoGP legend is nicknamed 'The Doctor?'
2. True or False: Mike Hailwood won the George Medal for bravery in 1973 after he collided with Clay Regazzoni during a Formula One Race and ran back to pull his fellow driver from his burning car?
3. How many years in a row did Mick Doohan win the 500cc Grand Prix World Championship?
4. The Tornamona was a former fishing boat which ran aground and sank in May 1985. Which famous rider was rescued, along with twelve other passengers, by the Portaferry Lifeboat?
5. In which race did Giacomo Agostini secure his last win?
6. Can you name the Spanish motorcycling legend who was born on 25th January 1947 in Zamora?
7. Who is the only person to have won Grand Prix World Championships on both two and four wheels?
8. How many times was Stefan Everts a Motocross World Champion?
9. Who was suspended by the FIM for six months in 1956 for supporting a riders' strike after demands for more starting money had been refused?
10. True or False: Marc Coma won the Dakar Rally a record five times?

Quiz 6: Motorcycling Records

1. Who set the first official FIM motorcycle land speed record when he rode an Indian on Daytona Beach at 104.12mph (167.56km/h) in 1920?
2. Where did New Zealander Burt Munro set a speed record of 183mph (295km/h) for a motorcycle with an engine under 1000cc in 1967?
3. Who set the record for the World's fastest ever motorcycle wheelie when he hit a speed of 191.3mph (307.87km/h) in 1999?
4. What record was set by Tom Wiberg of Sweden when he created the Smalltoe in 2003 and rode it for 32.8 feet (10 metres)?
5. How many backflips did Travis Pastrana achieve in 30 seconds during a taping of Nitro Circus, the adrenaline-filled X Games style event, in 2008?
6. True or False: On 16th October 2010, Moroccan Mustafa Danguir rode a Suzuki RM125 across a 3-centimetre-wide wire rope 200 metres above the ground in Benidorm, Spain, to set the record for the World's highest motorcycle tightrope ride?
7. Which motorcycle sold for 1.35million US dollars at a Hollywood memorabilia auction in 2014?
8. Which two records did Robbie Maddison achieve when he tackled the Teahupo'o in Tahiti on a specially adapted KTM450 in 2015?
9. To the nearest ten, how many men did the ACS Tornadoes Motorcycle Team get on a 500cc Royal Enfield motorcycle in November 2017 to set the record for the most people on a moving motorcycle?
10. How many donuts did Mark Van Driel complete when he set the record for most donuts in one minute in September 2022?

Quiz 7: Great Rides (1)

1. In which US State would you be if you were riding around the Buffalo National River in the Ozark Mountains?
2. The Cabot Trail, named after the 15th century explorer John Cabot, can be found in which country?
3. To the nearest ten, how many hairpins are there on the north-east side of the Stelvio Pass in Italy?
4. True or False: The ride from Queenstown to Milford Sound is on the North Island of New Zealand?
5. Copper Canyon is a great ride in which country?
6. What is the name of the 800-mile highway that runs from Lhasa, the capital of Tibet, to Kathmandu, the capital of Nepal?
7. The ride from Peso Do Regua to Porto in Portugal follows which river?
8. The Natchez Trace Parkway is a 450-mile ride from Natchez, Mississippi to which city?
9. In which UK National Park would you find the Cat and Fiddle Road?
10. In which country would you find the Swartberg Pass?

Quiz 8: Great Rides (2)

1. The Big Sur Highway is in which US State?
2. True or False: The Sloc is a hill on the Isle of Man TT Course?
3. The famous twelve apostles' sea stacks can be found along which popular ride in Southern Australia?
4. The Karakoram Highway links which two Asian countries?
5. In which country would you be if you were riding the eleven sharp hairpin bends of the Trollstigen mountain pass?
6. In which US State would you find the Dalton Highway considered to be one of the World's most dangerous roads?
7. True or False: The ride from Chiang Mai to Pai in Thailand features 762 turns?
8. Transalpina is the highest road in which European country?
9. What is the name of the 144-mile route connecting Lake Louise in Banff National Park with Jasper in Jasper National Park through the Canadian Rockies?
10. A ride to the Cañon del Colca, one of the World's deepest canyons, would find you in which South American country?

Quiz 9: Miscellany (1)

1. What stunt did trials rider, Dougie Lampkin, achieve on the Isle of Man in September 2016?
2. Which street circuit in Belgium has hosted a round of the International Road Racing Championship (IRRC) since 2010?
3. What type of books would you associate with the author Bill Hufnagle, also known as 'Biker Billy?'
4. How many times did Colin Edwards win the Superbike World Championship?
5. What was the nickname of Steve Hislop?
6. Which circuit hosted the first ever live outside broadcast of a motorsport event anywhere in Britain, when the BBC cameras televised its annual races in 1955?
7. Which brand of motorcycle is also the name of a capital city?
8. Who had a Norton 500 motorcycle called 'La Poderosa' (The Mighty One)?
9. Which country hosted the Speedway of Nations event in 2022?
10. True or False: 2023 Dakar Rally winner Kevin Benavides raced for the Monster Energy Honda Team at the event?

Quiz 10: Anagrams – Circuits

Can you name the circuit from the anagram?

1. UGAI.
2. ONDRDDU.
3. UGAANL AECS.
4. WOIBLNL.
5. EASNS.
6. UOLEMLG.
7. ULAP AIDCRR.
8. ARTAIM.
9. IIHLPLP ADLISN.
10. EELNASLF IUANNOMT UERCSO.

SESSION 2: TRACK RACING

Quiz 1: MotoGP (1)

1. In what year was the Motorcycling World Championship rebranded to MotoGP?
2. In which country would you find the Buriram International Circuit?
3. Which tyre manufacturer claimed its first MotoGP win when Makoto Tamada won the 2004 Brazilian GP?
4. Which country hosted the first ever MotoGP night race in 2008?
5. What piece of technology was banned at the start of the 2010 season?
6. How many rounds of MotoGP were held in Spain in 2010?
7. What did the "rookie rule," in force between 2010 and 2013, prevent a newcomer from doing?
8. At which circuit did Marco Simoncelli suffer a fatal accident during the 2011 season?
9. Which manufacturer joined the premier class with a factory-supported team for the first time at the start of the 2017 season?
10. To the nearest ten, how many Grand Prix World Championship races did Valentino Rossi start during his career?

Quiz 2: MotoGP (2)

1. Can you name the two British riders who competed in every round of the 2004 MotoGP season?
2. Who won the last two races of the 2005 MotoGP season?
3. True or False: Álex Marquez is the older brother of Marc Márquez?
4. Who won the Czech Republic MotoGP in the 2014 season?
5. Which manufacturer won its first Grand Prix World Championship since 2000 when Joan Mir won the title in 2020?
6. True or False: 2021 Champion Fabio Quartararo is the first French rider to win a premier class championship?
7. How many rounds were there in the 2022 MotoGP season?
8. What devices were banned from MotoGP in 2023?
9. Which two countries were added to the MotoGP calendar at the start of the 2023 season?
10. What is the maximum number of tyres a rider is permitted to use during a MotoGP round in the 2023 season?

Quiz 3: MotoGP (3)

1. Can you name the British rider who won the 125cc race at the British MotoGP round in the 2008 season?
2. Which class was replaced by Moto2 in 2010?
3. Can you name the rider who died during Moto2 practice at the Catalan Grand Prix in 2016 after a high-speed impact with his own stricken bike?
4. Which manufacturer replaced Honda as the sole supplier of Moto2 engines in 2019?
5. For which team did Andrea Iannone race during the 2019 MotoGP season?
6. Who won the opening race of the 2022 MotoGP season in Qatar?
7. Who achieved a speed of 225mph (363km/h) at the 2022 Italian MotoGP?
8. True or False: Moto3 riders cannot be older than twenty-eight?
9. Which rider won the 2022 Moto3 World Championship?
10. Who won the first Moto2 race of the 2023 season in Portugal?

Quiz 4: GP World Championship - {Pre-MotoGP} (1)

1. In what year was the inaugural season of the FIM Motorcycling World Championships?
2. What was the Italian Grand Prix known as until 1990?
3. How many World titles did Giacomo Agostini win?
4. Which country hosted the first World Championship race outside of Europe?
5. What was special about Geoffrey Nash's win at the 500cc Yugoslavian Grand Prix in 1969?
6. Who was the 500cc Grand Prix World Champion in both 1973 and 1974?
7. Which two riders won all 500cc races for the 1983 season between them?
8. True or False: Push starts were banned at the start of the 1987 season?
9. Who was left paralysed following a crash at Mizano in 1994?
10. Who was the first Spanish rider to win the 500cc class?

Quiz 5: GP World Championship {Pre-MotoGP} (2)

1. Which manufacturer provided the bike for Libero Liberati when he won the title in the 1957 season?
2. Who gave Honda their first World title when he won the 125cc championship in 1961?
3. True or False: Mike Hailwood won ten out of twelve races in the 250cc class during the 1966 season?
4. Why had Honda, Suzuki, and Yamaha all withdrawn from the sport by the end of 1968?
5. Which manufacturer helped Ángel Nieto secure his first five World titles?
6. What nationality was 1972 250cc World Champion, Jarno Saarinen?
7. Who are the only father and son to win the 500cc World Championship?
8. True or False: Carlo Ubbiali won the 250cc World title six times?
9. Which class was dropped at the end of the 1982 season?
10. Which happened first: a World Championship race in Asia or a World Championship race in North America?

Quiz 6: World Superbikes (1)

1. In what year was the inaugural season of the FIM Superbike World Championship?
2. How many times did Carl Fogarty win the Superbike World title?
3. Who won the last nine races of the 2002 Superbike World Championship to claim the title?
4. Who was the first Frenchman to win the title?
5. How many points separated James Toseland in first and Noriyuku Haga in second at the end of the 2007 season?
6. Which circuit replaced Vallelunga on the calendar for the 2009 season?
7. Who won the most races during the 2016 season?
8. The Superpole Race, introduced in 2019, consists of how many laps?
9. Who won both races and the Superpole Race at MotorLand Aragon in the 2019 season?
10. Which tyre manufacturer is the exclusive tyre partner and supplier for the 2023 season?

Quiz 7: World Superbikes (2)

1. True or False: Steve Hislop won Race One at Donington Park in the 2001 season?
2. At which two circuits did Italian rider Lorenzo Lanzi win races during the 2005 season?
3. Which manufacturer took the constructors' title in 2007?
4. Who won both races at Silverstone in the 2010 season?
5. In which country would you find the Circuito San Juan Villicum?
6. Which two riders won the opening races of the 2013 season at Phillip Island?
7. How many races did Aprilia Racing Team – Red Devils riders Jordi Torres and Leon Haslam win between them during the 2015 season?
8. Can you name the Spanish rider who represented the Orelac Racing Verdnatura Team during the 2021 season?
9. What nationality is 2021 champion, Toprak Razgatlioğlu?
10. How many points are awarded to the winner of a race (excluding the Superpole Race) in the 2023 season?

Quiz 8: Sidecar World Championship

1. Can you name the driver who won four of the first five Sidecar World Championships?
2. Who was passenger to Fritz Schneidegger when he won the Sidecar World title in 1966 and 1967?
3. Which manufacturer won the Sidecar World constructors' title every year from 1977 to 1988?
4. How many times did Rolf Biland win the Sidecar World Championship?
5. The Seymaz, used by George O'Dell to win the 1977 championship, was noted for having what type of steering?
6. Which sidecar pairing suffered a massive crash at the 1985 Dutch TT at Assen causing them to miss most of the season?
7. What nickname do Australians give to a sidecar passenger?
8. What is the name of the founder of the Swiss Sidecar manufacturer, LCR?
9. Who was the passenger when Tim Reeves won the Sidecar World title in 2007?
10. True or False: Kirsi Kainulainen became the first female motorcycle World Champion when she was passenger to Pekka Päivärinta in 2016?

Quiz 9: British Superbikes (1)

1. Who won the inaugural season of British Superbikes (BSB)?
2. How many times did Steve Hislop win the BSB title?
3. What disease was James Whitham diagnosed with whilst leading the standings in the 1995 season?
4. Which team was Tommy Hill racing for when he won the 2011 BSB title?
5. Up to 2022, who is the only Spanish rider to win the BSB title?
6. Which company took over the responsibility for the organisation and promotion of the British Superbike Championship in 2008?
7. True or False: Shayne Byrne has won the BSB title eight times?
8. Which European circuit hosted a round of British Superbikes every year from 2012 to 2019?
9. Who won all three races in the opening round of BSB at Silverstone National in 2022?
10. Which two TV channels screened live coverage of the BSB Championship in the United Kingdom during the 2023 season?

Quiz 10: British Superbikes (2)

1. On which BSB circuit would you find the corners: Gooseneck, Hairpin, Charlies, and Coppice?
2. John Reynolds and Steve Hislop won all but two races in the 2001 BSB season between them. Which two riders won the other two races?
3. What forced the abandonment of the day's races at Brands Hatch on 6th April 2008?
4. What did the Evolution class replace in 2010?
5. How many times have Norton won the British Superbike Constructors title?
6. Can you name the Japanese rider who won his third BSB title in the 2010 season?
7. Which manufacturer was represented by riders Christian Iddon and Christophe Ponsson during the 2014 BSB season?
8. Who won both races at Knockhill during the 2017 BSB season?
9. Due to the Coronavirus pandemic the 2020 BSB season was shortened to six rounds. Can you name four of the six circuits that hosted a round?
10. What nationality is Bjorn Estment, who raced for the Powerslide/Catfoss Racing Team in the 2022 season?

SESSION 3: ROAD RACING

Quiz 1: North-West 200 (1)

1. In what year was the North-West 200 first held?
2. What is the name of the street circuit used for the event?
3. To the nearest mile, how long is the circuit?
4. Who recorded the first 100mph lap of the course on a Norton 500cc in 1957?
5. What is the name of the roundabout between University Corner and Mather's Cross?
6. Who won the 350cc and 500cc races at the 1961 North-West 200?
7. Which club has been the organiser of the event since 1964?
8. How many races did John Williams win at the 1974 meeting?
9. Can you name the three riders who died on "Black Saturday" in 1979?
10. True or False: Eddy Laycock won both 250cc races at the 1990 event?

Quiz 2: North-West 200 (2)

1. Who won three races at the 1999 meeting?
2. In which race did Alastair Seeley claim his first win at the North-West?
3. Which manufacturer claimed its first North-West 200 win at the 2010 meeting?
4. What caused significant delays to the 2011 meeting before it was eventually cancelled due to an extensive oil spill on the track?
5. True or False: In 2012, John McGuinness set a fastest ever recorded speed on the North-West circuit of 208mph (335km/h)?
6. How many wins did Robert Dunlop record at the event?
7. What placed the 2023 meeting at risk of being cancelled?
8. At which section of the course did Lee Johnston come off his machine during practice for the 2023 races?
9. Which team were forced to withdraw during the 2023 meeting "due to no confidence in the application of the Superstock technical regulations?"
10. Can you name the American newcomer who finished seventh in Supertwin Race Two at the 2023 meeting?

Quiz 3: Ulster Grand Prix

1. In what year was the Ulster Grand Prix first held?
2. What was the name of the original 20.5-mile circuit used for the event during the first 17 years of its existence?
3. In 1953, the race moved to the current circuit. What is that called?
4. To the nearest mile, what is the distance of the current circuit?
5. How many times did Geoff Duke win the 500cc race at the Ulster GP?
6. True or False: Jim Redman won the 350cc race every year between 1961 and 1964?
7. Who won the 50cc race at both the 1969 and 1970 events?
8. What caused the cancellation of the event in 1972?
9. True or False: The hairpin on the course is known as the 'Lindsay Hairpin?'
10. How many Ulster GP races did Joey Dunlop win?

Quiz 4: Macau Motorcycle Grand Prix

1. In what year was the Macau Motorcycle GP first held?
2. What is the name of the circuit used for the event?
3. To the nearest mile, how long is the circuit?
4. Who, in 1976, became the first British winner of the race?
5. Up to 2022, how many times has Michael Rutter won the race?
6. What bike was Glenn Irwin riding when he won the event in 2017?
7. True or False: John McGuinness has never won in Macau?
8. What is the name of the corner at the end of the main straight?
9. Up to 2022, which Dunlop is the only one to have won in Macau?
10. Can you name the Finnish rider who won the 2022 race?

Quiz 5: Manx Grand Prix (1)

1. In what year was the Manx Grand Prix (MGP), or Manx Amateur Road Races as it was initially known, first held?
2. Which entity organises the Manx Grand Prix?
3. Who is the most successful rider in the history of the Manx Grand Prix, with eleven wins?
4. The A.B. Crookall Trophy is awarded to the winner of which race?
5. True or False: There are no sidecar races in the Manx Grand Prix?
6. Who, in 1989, became the first woman to compete at the Manx Grand Prix?
7. Over how many laps of the Snaefell Mountain Course is the Senior Manx Grand Prix race contested?
8. Who won the 1949 Senior MGP?
9. Can you name the Manx rider who suffered a fatal accident at Ballaugh Bridge whilst leading the 2004 Junior MGP?
10. Which race was discontinued prior to the 2022 Manx Grand Prix?

Quiz 6: Manx Grand Prix (2)

1. Where did Phil Hogg crash whilst leading the 1988 Senior MGP?
2. In what year did Braddan Bridge House, home of the Joey Dunlop Foundation, host is first guest for the Manx Grand Prix?
3. What prevented the Senior MGP race from being held in 2007?
4. What feat did Carolyn Sells achieve in the Ultra-Lightweight race at the 2009 Manx Grand Prix?
5. The Douglas Pirie Trophy is awarded to the winner of which race?
6. Who won the Lightweight race at the 2016 Manx Grand Prix?
7. In 1976, PC Denis Hamer was killed on duty after being struck by a motorbike in the Junior Race. Where did the incident occur?
8. True or False: Eighteen nations were represented at the 2018 Manx Grand Prix?
9. How many races did Nathan Harrison win at the 2019 Manx Grand Prix?
10. Which race was won by Rob Hodson at the 2022 Manx Grand Prix?

Quiz 7: Classic TT (2013-2019)

1. Who won the Senior Classic 500cc race at the 2013 Classic TT?
2. Which race did John McGuinness and Giacomo Agostini recreate at the 2013 Classic TT?
3. What did Ramsey Hairpin commentator, Roy Moore, describe the sound of the Moto Guzzi as during the inaugural Classic TT races?
4. Which manufacturer was honoured with a special parade lap at the 2015 Classic TT?
5. Who won the Junior Classic 350cc race in 2015 and 2017?
6. What does VMCC stand for?
7. True or False: In 2016, Bruce Anstey set an outright Classic TT lap record of 17 minutes 45.348 seconds (127.496mph) on a Yamaha YZR500?
8. Who came back from 18 months out injured to win the 2018 Senior Classic 500cc race?
9. The 2019 Classic TT featured a demonstration lap in honour of which TT legend?
10. How many races did Dean Harrison win during the Classic TT years?

Quiz 8: Southern 100 Road Races

1. What is the name of the course used for the annual Southern 100 Road Races?
2. In what year were the Southern 100 Road Races first held?
3. In which town on the Isle of Man would you find the start/finish line of the Southern 100 course?
4. What is the name of the church located at Church Bends?
5. With thirty-two wins, after the 2022 meeting, who is the most successful rider in the history of the Southern 100?
6. What position in the organising committee was held by Peter Oates at the 2019 races?
7. In what year were Sidecar races introduced into the event?
8. Who, in 1989, achieved the first 100mph lap of the course?
9. Manxman, Derek Ennett, has the honour of being the winner of the first race held, what was the engine capacity (cc) of the machine he was riding during that race?
10. Who set an outright lap record for the Southern 100 course, with a time of 2 minutes 12.231 seconds (115.707mph), during the 2017 Solo Championship race?

Quiz 9: Scarborough

1. What is the name of the circuit at Scarborough?
2. In what year was the circuit opened?
3. Which section of the course was introduced in 1991 to reduce speeds through the start and finish?
4. Who won the Gold Cup Race every year between 2003 and 2009?
5. True or False: The circuit is 3.82 miles long?
6. Who won both Senior races at the 2017 Cock O' The North meeting?
7. How many races did Derek Shiels win at the 2022 Gold Cup meeting?
8. True or False: Ian Lougher has taken more than 130 wins at Scarborough during his career?
9. The rise after the Mere Hairpin is named after which legendary rider?
10. Who won the Bob Smith Spring Cup feature race in 2023?

Quiz 10: Other Irish Road Races

1. Which race meeting first took place on Saturday 19th April 1958?
2. Which two races did Michael Browne win at the 2023 Cookstown 100?
3. Who won the Carole Nash Grand Final race at the 2019 Munster 100?
4. Which race takes place on the Crossakiel Circuit?
5. Can you name the four riders that made up the Armoy Armada, established in 1977?
6. To the nearest mile, how long is the circuit at Tandragee?
7. In what year did William Dunlop crash fatally during practice for the Skerries Road Races?
8. True or False: the two-day meeting at Walderstown, which started in the year 2000, is known as the "Race of the South?"
9. Who was the Rider of the Meeting at the 2022 Faugheen 50 Road Race?
10. In 2009, Dublin Corner at Skerries was renamed after which fallen rider?

SESSION 4: ISLE OF MAN TT (1)

Quiz 1: Isle of Man TT - General (1)

1. What does TT stand for?
2. What course was used for the first TT race in 1907?
3. Who was the winner of that first TT race?
4. In what year were travelling marshals introduced to the TT?
5. Who holds the record for the most TT wins?
6. What is the time gap between starters?
7. Can you name the first woman to compete at the TT and the race she took part in?
8. Which position in the organising committee has been held by Gary Thompson since 2012?
9. How many sidecar TT's has Dave Molyneux won?
10. Which four events have prevented the races from being held?

Quiz 2: Isle of Man TT: 1907-1914

1. How many competitors entered the first TT race on 28th May 1907?
2. What prize money was awarded to the winner of that first TT race?
3. Who achieved an average speed of 40.49mph, the first 40mph-plus race average, on his way to winning the single-cylinder class at the 1908 TT?
4. On which road was the start line of the first race held on the Snaefell Mountain Course?
5. Who won the 1911 Junior TT?
6. What did Frank Philipp achieve, whilst riding a two-stroke Scott, during the 1911 Senior TT?
7. Why did several manufacturers threaten to boycott the 1912 TT?
8. The seven-lap Senior race at the 1913 TT was held over two different days, who crashed fatally at Keppel Gate whilst leading the second leg?
9. What was made compulsory at the 1914 TT?
10. Can you name the two riders who finished first and second in the 1914 Junior TT who shared the same surname but were not related?

Quiz 3: Isle of Man TT: 1920s

1. In which race did Stanley Woods take his first TT win?
2. Who won the 1920 Senior TT?
3. Who, in 1921, became the only rider to ever win the Senior TT on a Junior machine?
4. What feat did Tom Sheard achieve when he won the 1922 Junior TT?
5. How many outfits lined up for the first ever Sidecar TT race?
6. Which pairing won that first Sidecar race?
7. What caused Wal Handley to slip off his bike at Signpost Corner during the 1925 Lightweight TT?
8. In what position did Jimmie Guthrie finish in the 1927 Senior TT?
9. Who won the 1928 Junior TT?
10. Where did Wal Handley, Jimmy Simpson, Jack Arnott, and Doug Lamb all crash during the 1929 Senior TT, with the latter succumbing to his injuries on the way to Nobles Hospital?

Quiz 4: Isle of Man TT: 1930s

1. What forced Charlie Dodson to retire at Kirk Michael on lap three of the 1930 Lightweight TT race?
2. Which company became the first to broadcast racing at the TT when they covered part of the 1930 Senior TT race?
3. Who won both the Junior and Senior races at the 1931 TT?
4. Which member of the British Royal Family watched the 1932 Senior TT from the Grandstand and Creg-Ny-Baa?
5. True or False: Stanley Woods won the Senior TT every year between 1932 and 1935?
6. In which race did Freddie Frith take his first TT win?
7. What feat was achieved by Italian, Omobono Tenni, in the 1937 Lightweight TT?
8. How many TT races did Jimmie Guthrie win during his career?
9. Who won the 1938 Lightweight TT?
10. Where did the Austrian, Karl Gall, suffer a fatal crash during practice for the 1939 TT?

Quiz 5: Isle of Man TT: 1947-1959 (1)

1. Why were speeds lower at the 1947 TT than the pre-war races?
2. Who won the 1947 Senior TT?
3. How many riders entered the 1948 TT?
4. Where did Les Graham retire during the 1948 Senior TT?
5. Who won the Clubman's Senior TT at the 1949 TT?
6. Who suffered a fatal accident at the 11th Milestone during the 1949 Junior TT race?
7. What was the time gap between the winner, Dario Ambrosini, and second place Maurice Cann, in the 1950 Lightweight TT race?
8. Who won the 1950 Junior TT?
9. Which race was won by Cromie McCandless at the 1951 TT?
10. In what year did the TT first host the British round of the Grand Prix Motorcycle World Championships?

Quiz 6: Isle of Man TT: 1947-1959 (2)

1. True or False: The winner of the 1952 and 1953 Lightweight TT races, Fergus Anderson, was named on the Nazis' "most wanted" list drawn up prior to their invasion of Britain?
2. Who won the Junior and Senior races at the 1953 TT?
3. What race was reintroduced at the 1954 TT and held on the 10.70-mile Clypse Course until 1959?
4. Which race did Philip Palmer win, riding a BSA, at the 1954 TT?
5. Who won the 1955 Junior TT?
6. How many TT races did John Surtees win during his career?
7. Which two races did Italian, Carlo Ubbiali, win at the 1956 TT?
8. Who was the first rider to lap the mountain course at over 100mph, on his way to winning the 1957 Senior TT?
9. True or False: The German, Walter Schneider, won four races at the Isle of Man TT?
10. In which race did MV Agusta take their first TT victory?

Quiz 7: Isle of Man TT: 1960s (1)

1. In what year did Manx Radio first broadcast coverage of the TT Races?
2. Who won the Lightweight 250cc race at the 1960 TT?
3. Which driver took his first TT win in the Sidecar race at the 1960 TT?
4. Which three races did Mike Hailwood win at the 1961 TT?
5. How many TT races did Phil Read win during his career?
6. Where did Tom Phillis suffer a fatal crash during the 1962 Junior TT, whilst lying in third position in the race?
7. Which manufacturer took their first TT victory in the two-lap 50cc race at the 1962 TT?
8. Who won the Lightweight 125cc race at the 1962 TT?
9. Who, in 1963, became the first Japanese rider to win a TT race?
10. In which race did John Surtees take his last TT win?

Quiz 8: Isle of Man TT: 1960s (2)

1. Who won both the Lightweight 250cc and Junior races at the 1963 TT?
2. Why did Mike Hailwood miss the 1964 Junior TT?
3. Where did Giacomo Agostini slide off his MV Agusta during a wet 1965 Senior TT?
4. Why was the 1966 TT postponed to September?
5. True or False: BMW drivers won every sidecar TT race held in the 1960s?
6. Who won the Production 750cc race at the 1967 TT, which had been reintroduced to mark the Diamond Jubilee?
7. What caused Giacomo Agostini's retirement from the 1967 Senior TT?
8. Who, in 1968, became the first rider to lap the mountain course at over 100mph on a 125cc machine?
9. Who won the last ever 50cc race at the 1968 TT?
10. Which manufacturer took their first TT victory in the 1969 Lightweight 125cc race?

Quiz 9: Isle of Man TT: 1970s (1)

1. In which race did Mick Grant take his first TT win?
2. Who won the Lightweight 250cc race at the 1970 TT?
3. Which pairing won the Sidecar 500cc race at the 1970 TT?
4. Who made his one and only TT appearance in the Lightweight 125cc race at the 1971 TT?
5. Who won the 1971 Junior TT?
6. Can you name the Italian rider who suffered a fatal accident during the 1972 Ultra-Lightweight race prompting Giacomo Agostini to announce that he would never return to the Isle of Man to race?
7. Who won the 1973 Senior TT?
8. How many races did Sidecar driver, Siegfried Schauzu, win during his TT career?
9. Tommy Robb's last ever race at the TT provided his only victory. Which race did he win?
10. Who won the 1974 Formula 750 Classic TT?

Quiz 10: Isle of Man TT: 1970s (2)

1. The Production race at the 1975 TT was held over how many laps of the mountain course?
2. Who won the 1975 Junior TT?
3. What caused Tony Rutter's retirement on the fifth lap of the Classic TT race at the 1975 TT?
4. How many TT races did Tom Herron win during his career?
5. Which pairing won the 1976 Production race?
6. Joey Dunlop's first TT victory came at the 1977 races. Which race did he win?
7. Who won the Formula Two race three years in a row between 1977 and 1979?
8. Who crashed on the last lap of the 1978 Senior TT at Bishopscourt, after setting a new lap record of 113.83mph, and would never race again due to his injuries?
9. Which pairing won both Sidecar legs at the 1979 TT?
10. Which two races did Mike Hailwood win after he made a comeback to the TT in 1978?

SESSION 5: ISLE OF MAN TT (2)

Quiz 1: Isle of Man TT: 1980s (1)

1. Who won the 1980 Senior TT?
2. Which pairing won both Sidecar legs at the 1981 TT?
3. In what year did Joey Dunlop first emulate Mike Hailwood's feat of winning three TT races in a week?
4. Who won the 1982 Formula One TT?
5. In what position did spouses, Dennis and Julia Bingham, finish in the Sidecar 1st Leg at the 1983 TT?
6. In which race did Mick Grant take his last TT win?
7. Which driver won his first Sidecar TT in the 2nd Leg at the 1983 TT, after 14 years of trying?
8. Who, in 1984, became the first American to win a TT?
9. Where did Graeme McGregor crash on the first lap of the TT Formula One race in 1985?
10. In which race did Steve Hislop take his first TT win?

Quiz 2: Isle of Man TT: 1980s (2)

1. How many Formula Two races did Tony Rutter win during the 1980s?
2. The 1986 Sidecar TT Race B was won by the pairing of Nigel Rollason and Don Williams riding a 750cc Barton Phoenix engine. In which movie, starring David Essex, did that machine appear?
3. Who lost his life after being involved in a freak accident with a horse at Ballaugh Bridge during the 1986 Junior TT?
4. Where did Trevor Nation run out of petrol whilst leading the 1986 Senior TT?
5. In which race did Carl Fogarty claim his first TT win?
6. True or False: Dave Leach won the Production Class D races for three years in a row between 1986 and 1988?
7. Who set an absolute lap record of 119.08mph during the 1988 Senior TT, before his bike burst into flames between Creg-Ny-Baa and Brandish?
8. Who, in 1989, achieved the first lap at over 120mph?
9. Where did Phil Mellor suffer a fatal accident during the 1300cc Production race at the 1989 TT?
10. Which driver took his first TT win in Sidecar Race A at the 1989 TT?

Quiz 3: Isle of Man TT: 1990s (1)

1. In which race did Joey Dunlop equal Mike Hailwood's record of 14 TT wins?
2. Who pipped Steve Hislop by 1.8 seconds to win the 1990 Junior TT?
3. Who won both the Formula One and Senior races at the 1990 TT?
4. Who, in 1990, became the first man to lap the TT course at over 100mph on a Formula Two Sidecar?
5. Which pairing won both Sidecar races at the 1992 TT?
6. How many years had Norton gone without a Senior TT win before Steve Hislop claimed victory in the 1992 race?
7. What revolutionary bike did New Zealander, Shaun Harris, ride in the 1993 Formula One and Senior TT races?
8. Who took his first TT win in the Supersport 400 race at the 1993 TT?
9. Who crashed heavily on the exit from Ballaugh Bridge during the 1994 Formula One race, when his rear wheel collapsed?
10. At which corner did Phillip McCallen run out of fuel on the last lap of the 1994 Junior TT?

Quiz 4: Isle of Man TT: 1990s (2)

1. How many TT races did Iain Duffus win during his career?
2. Which pairing won both Sidecar races at the 1994 TT?
3. Who took his only TT win in the 1995 Ultra-Lightweight race, winning by just 0.6 seconds?
4. Which four races did Phillip McCallen win at the 1996 TT?
5. Who won the Singles TT for three years in a row between 1997 and 1999?
6. True or False: The 1997 Junior TT saw a first TT win for Ian Simpson?
7. What innovation was introduced at the 1997 Senior TT?
8. Who, in 1998, won a rain-soaked Lightweight TT which started as a three-lap race but was reduced to two laps as the opening lap was in progress?
9. Whose one-stop strategy in the 1998 Senior TT helped him claim second place on the podium?
10. Who crashed on Bray Hill on the first lap of the 1999 Formula One TT resulting in the race being red flagged?

Quiz 5: Isle of Man TT: 2000s (1)

1. Which three races did Joey Dunlop win at the 2000 TT?
2. In July 2000, Dunlop was tragically killed during a relatively unknown road race meeting, held in which country?
3. Which race did Manxman, Richard 'Milky' Quayle, win at the 2002 TT?
4. Which TT legend presented David Jefferies with the Senior TT trophy in 2002?
5. Which manufacturer claimed their first TT victory in nearly three decades when Bruce Anstey won the 2003 Junior TT?
6. Can you name the Isle of Man resident who took his first win in the 2003 Ultra-Lightweight TT?
7. Who won both the Production 600cc and Production 1000cc races at the 2003 TT?
8. How many TT races did David Jefferies win before his tragic death at the 2003 TT?
9. In which race did Ryan Farquhar take his first TT win?
10. Can you name the motorcycle journalist who was involved in a fatal collision with a marshal on lap two of the 2005 Senior TT at the exit of Kirk Michael village?

Quiz 6: Isle of Man TT: 2000s (2)

1. At which TT did John McGuinness become the first rider to complete a lap at over 130mph?
2. Which pairing won both Sidecar races at the 2006 TT?
3. In which race did Ian Hutchinson take his first TT win?
4. Who won the 2008 Superbike TT race?
5. Where did Sammy Miller crash his twin-cylinder 1978 Ducati 900SS during the parade lap at the 2008 TT?
6. Which manufacturer celebrated their fiftieth year of racing at the TT in 2009?
7. Who won the Pro Class in the inaugural TTXGP race for electric bikes?
8. In which race did Michael Dunlop claim his first TT win?
9. Who won the 2009 Senior TT?
10. How many TT wins has Sidecar passenger, Dan Sayle, taken during his TT career?

Quiz 7: Isle of Man TT: 2010s (1)

1. In what year did the Birchall Brothers take their first win in a Sidecar TT race?
2. How many races did Ian Hutchinson win at the 2010 TT?
3. Who crashed at the Verandah during the 2010 Senior TT?
4. Who won the 2010 TT Zero race?
5. Who took his first TT win in the 2011 Supersport Junior TT Race Two?
6. The Senior TT was cancelled in 2012 for the first time in its history. What caused the cancellation?
7. Who won the inaugural 650cc Supertwin race, held under the banner of the Lightweight TT, at the 2012 races?
8. Up to 2022, how many TT wins has Bruce Anstey taken during his career?
9. Can you name the TV presenter who completed a lap of the course on a sidecar outfit built entirely from Meccano at the 2013 TT?
10. True or False: Michael Dunlop won four races at TT 2013 and repeated the feat a year later?

Quiz 8: Isle of Man TT: 2010s (2)

1. Where did Jonathan Howarth crash on lap one of the 2013 Senior TT, resulting in the race being red flagged?
2. Who, at TT 2014, became the first father and son duo to win races in different classes during the same race week?
3. Which manufacturer won the TT Zero race every year between 2014 and 2019?
4. Can you name the rally driver who set a lap record on four wheels with a time of 17 minutes 49.75seconds (average speed of 126.971mph) driving a ProDrive-prepared Subaru WRX STI during TT 2016?
5. Who was the owner of Team Traction Control, which won four races across TT 2015 and TT 2016?
6. Who won the Lightweight race at both the 2015 and 2016 TT Races?
7. What bike did Ian Lougher ride during the Superbike and Senior races at TT 2016 and TT 2018?
8. Which two races did Ian Hutchinson win at the 2017 TT?
9. Who was involved in an accident with a course car during a suspended qualifying session at TT 2018?
10. In 2019, for the first time ever, five races were held on one day. Which ones?

Quiz 9: Isle of Man TT: 2022

1. How many races did Glenn Irwin enter at TT 2022?
2. Which Olympic gold medallist joined the commentary team on TT+, the new live streaming service?
3. Can you name the two riders who crashed at Laurel Bank during the Monday and Tuesday qualifying sessions?
4. What caused Davey Todd to retire on lap two of the 2022 Superbike TT race?
5. True or False: Michael Dunlop won both Supersport races at TT 2022 and took his total TT wins to twenty-two?
6. Who finished third in the Supertwin TT Race?
7. In what position did Ryan and Callum Crowe finish in Sidecar Race Two?
8. Which rider took part in every race at TT 2022, including the sidecar?
9. Who suffered two bird strikes during the 2022 Senior TT?
10. What is the name of the FHO team owner?

Quiz 10: Isle of Man TT - General (2)

1. Which town holds a popular drag sprint event during the festival?
2. Who was the first TT rider to lose his life in an accident on the Snaefell Mountain Course?
3. In what month do the races traditionally start?
4. What nickname was given to the late Gwen Crellin, a TT marshal, by Giacomo Agostini?
5. Which charitable organisation provides accommodation for people with disabilities at Braddan Bridge House?
6. How many digital red flags were placed around the Snaefell Mountain Course prior to TT 2022?
7. Which Isle of Man brewery produces Wheelie-Konni's Weissbier, named after well-known TT superfan, Konrad Ammenhauser?
8. Can you name the late Manx Radio TT commentator who was associated with the phrase, "the roads are strangely quiet?"
9. In what year were morning practice sessions discontinued?
10. Where on the island would you find a statue to Steve Hislop?

SESSION 6: DISCIPLINES AND EVENTS

Quiz 1: Enduro (1)

1. True or False: The International Six Days Enduro was first held in 1913 at Carlisle, England?
2. How many times did David Knight win the E3 class in the FIM Enduro World Championship?
3. Which country hosted the International Six Days Enduro in 2006?
4. Which event was founded in the United States in 1975 by Dave Coombs?
5. Of the eight events in the 2007 FIM Enduro World Championship, six were held in Europe, one was held in the United States, where was the other one held?
6. True or False: An all-female British team won the International Silver Vase at the 1927 International Six Days Enduro?
7. What brand of bike was the Australian Matthew Phillips riding when he won the E2 class of the FIM Enduro World Championships in 2016?
8. In which country is the Erzberg Rodeo held?
9. Who won the inaugural FIM Hard Enduro World Championship in 2018?
10. What is the maximum capacity for machines in the Enduro 1 (E1) class of the 2023 FIM Enduro World Championship?

Quiz 2: Enduro (2)

1. True or False: Hollywood actor Clint Eastwood represented the United States at the 1964 International Six Days Enduro?
2. What nationality was 1990 350cc four stroke Enduro World Champion, Otakar Kotrba?
3. Who won the Erzberg Rodeo five years in a row between 2007 and 2011?
4. How many times was Dick Burleson the AMA National Champion?
5. What brand of bike was Graham Jarvis riding when he won the 2013 Erzberg Rodeo?
6. Why were the French team initially disqualified from the 2015 International Six Days Enduro, only to be reinstated, then demoted to 23rd in the final standings later that year?
7. Can you name the Finnish rider who won the E1 class of the FIM Enduro World Championship in 2015 and 2016, and the E2 class in 2018?
8. Which country won the 2021 International Six Days Enduro?
9. Who won the 2022 FIM Hard Enduro World Championship?
10. Which country hosted two rounds of the 2022 FIM Enduro World Championship?

Quiz 3: Motocross

1. What is motocross also known as in the United Kingdom?
2. Which country hosted the first Motocross des Nations in 1947?
3. Which manufacturer claimed its first Motocross World Championship when Joël Robert won the 1970 250cc crown?
4. Who, in 1978, became the first non-European competitor to win a Motocross World Championship?
5. What did Doug Henry achieve in the AMA Motocross Championship in 1998?
6. What is the duration of a race in the FIM Motocross World Championship?
7. Who won the MXGP Motocross World Championship in 2014 and 2017?
8. How many times did Billy MacKenzie win the ACU British Motocross Championship?
9. Which country did Travis Pastrana represent at the 2018 Motocross des Nations?
10. Who won the women's MX Motocross World Championship in 2022?

Quiz 4: Speedway

1. Which country hosted the first national speedway championship in 1926?
2. Inaugurated in 1929, what was the forerunner of the Speedway World Championship known as?
3. Which stadium hosted the first Speedway World Final in 1936?
4. What is the maximum length of a speedway track?
5. What must a speedway motorcycle be fuelled by?
6. How many times did New Zealander Barry Briggs win the World Speedway title?
7. Who was Speedway European Champion in 2020?
8. In which country does the Alfred Smoczyk Memorial Event take place?
9. Who is the only German rider to become Speedway World Champion?
10. Which British speedway club won its 13th top tier league championship in 2022?

Quiz 5: Trials

1. In 1914, Frank Philip was the first winner of which British motorcycle trials competition?
2. What is the standard penalty for touching the ground with a foot in a trials event?
3. In which town has the Scottish Six Days Trial been based since 1977?
4. Which country hosted the first Trials des Nations in 1984?
5. How many FIM World Trial Outdoor titles did Jordi Tarrés win during his career?
6. Who joined Steve Colley, Dougie Lampkin, and Graham Jarvis to help Great Britain win the Trials des Nations in 2002?
7. Can you name the Japanese rider who was FIM Trial Outdoor World Champion in 2004?
8. What score is sometimes referred to as "a fiasco?"
9. True or False: Antoni Bou was the sole outdoor and indoor FIM Trial World Champion from 2007 to 2022?
10. Who won the 2019 Scottish Six Days Trial?

Quiz 6: Electric Bikes

1. Which company built a prototype electric motorcycle called the Papoose in 1967?
2. True or False: In 2011, Chip Yates set a Guinness record for the fastest electric motorcycle of 316.899km/h (196.912mph)?
3. How many times has Bruce Anstey won the Isle of Man TT Zero Race?
4. Which manufacturer released the first mass-produced electric scooter in 1996?
5. What caused the postponement of the start of the inaugural Moto-E World Cup in 2019?
6. Can you name the Italian rider who won that inaugural Moto-E World Cup?
7. Which circuit hosted the final round of the 2020 Moto-E World Cup?
8. Can you name the 2022 Moto-E World Cup winner who switched to World Superbikes for the 2023 season?
9. Which Italian firm entered its EVA Ribelle Streetfighter machine in the 2023 edition of the Super Hooligan National Championship in America?
10. True or False: The Moto-E bikes in the 2023 season have a top speed of 250km/h?

Quiz 7: Supermoto

1. Originally known as "Superbikers" which motorsport facility in Southern California held the event between 1980 and 1985?
2. In what year was the AMA Supermoto Championship founded?
3. Which manufacturer released the first factory produced Supermoto in 1991?
4. Who was the first winner of the FIM Supermoto World Championship?
5. Up to 2022, how many times has Thomas Chareyre been FIM Supermoto World Champion?
6. Who was the only rider to win the AMA Supermoto Championship twice?
7. Which company was the official tyre manufacturer for the FIM Supermoto World Championship between 2006 and 2010?
8. In what year did the AMA Supermoto Championship fold?
9. What brand of bike was Adrien Chareyre riding when he became FIM Supermoto World Champion in 2011?
10. Who was the FIM Supermoto World Champion in 2021 and 2022?

Quiz 8: Endurance World Championship

1. What is the shortest duration for an FIM Endurance World Championship race?
2. True or False: The most famous and prestigious endurance race, the Bol d'Or, was held for the first time in 1922 on a circuit near Toulouse?
3. Which British circuit hosted an endurance race in the inaugural season of the World Championship in 1960?
4. Can you name the British racer who won the 1996 Endurance World Championship?
5. How many times did Alex Vieira win the Endurance World title?
6. What bike was used by the Zongshen 2 Team to win the 2002 World title?
7. Can you name the four-time Endurance World Champion whose brother won the 2011 Superbike World Championship?
8. Which two Asian circuits hosted a round of the Endurance World Championship in 2019?
9. Which manufacturer won the Endurance World Championship race in the Czech Republic in October 2021?
10. For which team did Sylvain Guintoli race during the 2022 season?

Quiz 9: Dakar Rally

1. In what year was the Dakar Rally first held?
2. Who is credited as the founder and original organiser of the Dakar Rally?
3. What technology was used for the first time at the 1992 event?
4. Can you name the 1989 winner who died at the 1992 race following a collision with one of the organisation vehicles?
5. Which Spanish city hosted the start of the race in 1995, 1996, and 1999?
6. How many times did Cyril Despres win the Dakar Rally for bikes?
7. Why was the 2008 event cancelled?
8. Who won the 2018 edition of the Dakar Rally for bikes?
9. Which country hosted the race in 2019?
10. Can you name the Isle of Man TT rider who took on the Dakar Rally in 2023, finishing 80th?

Quiz 10: Pikes Peak International Hill Climb

1. In what year was the PPIHC first held?
2. What is the race also known as?
3. True or False: Harley Davidson have won the motorcycle class three times?
4. To the nearest mile, what is the race distance?
5. Who won the race four years in a row between 2000 and 2003?
6. To the nearest ten, how many turns are there on the course?
7. True or False: The PPIHC held in 2011 was the last time the course contained dirt sections?
8. Who was the first foreign winner of the motorcycle class?
9. Can you name the rider whose death at the 2019 race forced the organisation to postpone all motorcycle racing at the event?
10. What bike was Rennie Scaysbrook riding when he won the 2019 race?

SESSION 7: ENTERTAINMENT

Quiz 1: At the Movies (1)

1. Can you name the actor who was looking for a 'Cool Rider' in the 1982 movie, 'Grease 2?'
2. True or False: 'TT3D: Closer to the Edge' was filmed during the 2009 Isle of Man TT?
3. What is the name of the character played by Dennis Hopper in the 1969 movie, 'Easy Rider?'
4. "I need your clothes, your boots, and your motorcycle" is a line from which 1991 Arnold Schwarzenegger movie?
5. Can you name the New Zealand speed bike rider who is the focus of the 2005 movie 'The World's Fastest Indian' starring Anthony Hopkins?
6. 'The Grave Diggers Motorcycle Club' features in which 1974 Australian Cult Classic?
7. Who played the surly biker Johnny Strabler in the 1953 movie, 'The Wild One?'
8. 'Naked Under Leather' was the US title for which 1968 movie starring Marianne Faithfull?
9. 'Wild Hogs' is a 2007 movie about a biker gang on a road trip to California. Can you name the two actors who played Woody and Bobby?
10. In which Batman movie does the Batpod, Batman's chunky-wheeled bike, make its debut?

Quiz 2: At the Movies (2)

1. What brand and model of bike is disguised as a German BMW R75 in the 1963 movie, 'The Great Escape?'
2. Who plays Will Atkins, the alcoholic chief mechanic of Evel Knievel in the 1977 movie, 'Viva Knievel?'
3. Fill in the blanks to give the movie title: "Their credo is violence…their God is hate…and they call themselves ____ ____ ____?"
4. Which 2004 movie follows Che Guevara, played by Gael Garcia Bernal, as a newly qualified doctor with a motorbike and a hankering for the open road?
5. Who directed the 2007 movie, 'The Darjeeling Limited?'
6. Lightcycle bikes feature in which 2010 American science fiction action film?
7. Who narrated the 2015 documentary film, 'Hitting the Apex?'
8. Where were the motorcycle gang fronted by Vance, played by Willem Dafoe, heading for in the 1981 movie, The Loveless?
9. Can you name the actor who plays the devil, Mephistopheles, in the 2007 movie, 'Ghost Rider?'
10. 'Road,' a 2014 documentary film, tells the story of which famous motorcycling family?

Quiz 3: Celebrity Bikers

1. Can you name the 'Deadpool' actor who owns a rare Ducati Paul Smart Limited-Edition motorbike?
2. Which 'Lord of the Rings' actor owns a collection of both older and newer BMW's, including a custom-build S1000R?
3. True or False: Christian Bale hung up his helmet following the birth of his daughter and an accident on the track?
4. Which pop singer is married to motocrosser and freestyler, Carey Hart?
5. Actor John Abraham is an ambassador for which brand of motorcycle?
6. Can you name the actor who founded the Arch Motorcycle Company alongside Gard Hollinger in 2011?
7. Canadian singer Alanis Morissette is a massive fan of Ducati's, and she will be disappointed if you do not get the title to her first big hit because ___ ___ ___.
8. This actor would call you a fool if you tried to get him on a plane, but he would be happy if you offered him a motorbike. Who is he?
9. Can you name the 'Rebel Without a Cause' actor who rode a 1955 Triumph TR5 Trophy?
10. Which actor, who appeared in 'Inception' and 'The Dark Knight Rises,' made the news in 2017 for pursuing two young motorcycle thieves in Richmond, London?

Quiz 4: Literature

1. Who is the owner of the flying motorbike in 'Harry Potter and the Philosopher's Stone?'
2. On what island does Captain Corelli squire the beautiful Pelagia around on his motorbike in the novel, 'Captain Corelli's Mandolin?'
3. Who wrote, 'A Motorbike,' a poem about the aftermath of World War II?
4. 'Frank N' Stan's Bucket List' is a series of books by JC Williams that centre around the lead characters obsession with which motorcycle race?
5. Who was the author of the book, 'Hell's Angels: The Strange and Terrible Saga of the Outlaw Motorcycle Gangs,' published in 1967?
6. Which former MotoGP and World Superbike racer released the autobiography, 'Leathered: A life taken to extremes on and off the bike?'
7. 'Runaway Ralph,' the children's book by Beverly Cleary, sees Ralph take to the open road on his motorcycle. What type of creature is Ralph?
8. 'By Any Means: The Brand-New Adventure from Wicklow to Wollongong' is by which TV star, adventurer, and number one bestselling author?
9. Who said, "God didn't create metal so that man could make paper clips?"
10. The book 'Lone Rider' by Elspeth Beard tells her story as the first British woman to do what?

Quiz 5: Music (1)

1. Which word follows 'motorcycle' in the title of a 1992 song by the Manic Street Preachers?
2. 'Born to be Wild' by Steppenwolf features on the soundtrack of which cult 1960s movie?
3. According to George Formby, what was riding in the TT Races easier than?
4. Can you name the comedian who had a 1975 hit with 'Funky Moped?'
5. In the song 'Ride Like the Wind' by Christopher Cross to which country's border is the protagonist heading for?
6. Where were Talking Heads riding to in their 1985 hit?
7. Who wanted you to take a ride with him in his 2001 hit 'Ride Wit Me?'
8. Complete the lyric to give the song title, "Like a ___ ___ ___ ___, I'll be gone when the morning comes."
9. Which band recorded the song 'Motorcycle Man' in 1980?
10. What type of horse was the cowboy in the Bon Jovi song 'Wanted Dead or Alive' riding on?

Quiz 6: Music (2)

1. Which folk singer recorded 'The Motorcycle Song' in 1967?
2. In 1979, AC-DC were travelling on the Highway to where?
3. Who released the song 'On the Road Again' in 1980?
4. Graham Dunnell was the lead singer of which 1980s band known for its songs 'Box Hill or Bust' and 'Just for Kicks?'
5. In the 1982 George Thorogood and the Destroyers song, who could tell right away that the protagonist was 'Bad to the Bone?'
6. Who just wanted to "get on my bike and ride" in the 1989 song 'Ride?'
7. What was the name of the 'Leader of the Pack' in the 1964 song by The Shangri-Las?
8. In 2007, Twisted Angels released 'Indulgence' an official song to mark the centenary of which motorcycle race?
9. 'This Life' by Curtis Stigers and The Forest Rangers was the theme song for which 2000s TV series?
10. Which band sung about a 'Little Honda' in 1964?

Quiz 7: Television (1)

1. Which manufacturer provided the bikes for Ewan McGregor and Charley Boorman to complete their 19000-mile (31000km) journey from London to New York in the 'Long Way Round?'
2. Jesse Mach, played by Rex Smith, was the rider of which all-terrain attack motorcycle?
3. Can you name the ex-Manchester United player who took on an extreme motorcycle adventure in 'Into the Unknown?'
4. Dave Myers and Si King are better known as what?
5. True or False: In an episode of The Simpsons, Homer wins a Harley-Davidson and starts his own outlaw motorcycle club, naming it "Hell's Satans?"
6. 'Ride with Norman Reedus' is a popular bike show on Amazon Prime. Reedus is known for his role as Daryl Dixon in which long-running zombie apocalypse series?
7. Which channel aired the reality TV show 'Biker Build-Off' between 2002 and 2007?
8. Michiel Huisman played Walter Davidson in which 2016 American miniseries?
9. Which actor rode a red and silver BSA A65 'White Lightning' 650cc motorbike in the 1980s TV show, 'Boon?'
10. True or False: 'No Room for Error' is a 2023 TV documentary series about the North-West 200?

Quiz 8: Television (2)

1. Can you name the British motorcycle trials game show that aired on BBC One from 6th August 1979 to 17th August 1992?
2. True or False: Supermoto was originally conceived by Gavin Trippe in 1979 as a segment of the American TV show 'Wide World of Sports?'
3. What are the names of the father and son team who manufactured custom chopper-style motorcycles in the series 'American Chopper?'
4. Which motorcycle race features as the challenge for Guy in an episode of series two of 'Speed with Guy Martin?'
5. True or False: Brad Pitt appeared in an episode of 'Street Hawk?'
6. What bikes were used by Ewan McGregor and Charley Boorman for their TV series, 'Long Way Up,' first broadcast on Apple TV+ in 2020?
7. What were the late Jennifer Paterson and Clarissa Dickson Wright better known as in their BBC TV series?
8. A Francis Barnett Falcon F150 and a BSA Golden Flash 110 featured in which long-running British police soap set in 1960s North Riding of Yorkshire?
9. Who is the presenter of 'The Motorbike Show?'
10. In what year did Sky Sports show the start of the Isle of Man TT Formula One race live from the TT Grandstand?

Quiz 9: Video Games (1)

1. Roy Hubbard composed the music for two early motorcycle video games. Can you name them?
2. The sequel to which bike game went 'Super' in 1991?
3. Where were the Biker Mice from in the 1994 Super Nintendo game?
4. The name and likeness of which rider was licensed for three Supercross games published between 1998 and 2002?
5. Which company released the 'TT Superbikes' game on the PlayStation 2 in 2005?
6. Which hedgehog gets his hands on a motorcycle called the 'Dark Rider' in a 2005 game released by Sega?
7. In 2006, Polyphony Digital produced 'Tourist Trophy: The Real Road Racing Simulation' for the PlayStation 2. What racing game series is that developer more famous for?
8. Which motorcycle game, upon release in 2013, was considered by critics to be "one of the worst video games ever made?"
9. I.R.I.S. and S.P.I.K.E. are the names of two motorcycles found in which game developed by Twisted Pixel Games in 2014?
10. Which American developer and publisher produced the 'Dakar Desert Rally' video game in 2022?

Quiz 10: Video Games (2)

1. In which century is the 1985 Nintendo release 'Mach Rider' set?
2. Which company publishes the 'TT Isle of Man: Ride on the Edge' games?
3. The 'Hardy-Daytona' was the first motorcycle to appear in which video game series?
4. The 'Castrol Honda World Superbikes Team VTR' game was released exclusively on which platform?
5. What is the name of the biker gang led by Ben in the 1995 game 'Full Throttle?'
6. Since 2013, which developer has held the official license to produce MotoGP video games?
7. How many motocross racing games published by THQ were endorsed by Ricky Carmichael?
8. Which company is the publisher of the Trials racing video game series?
9. In which game does Dante acquire a motorcycle called the 'Cavaliere?'
10. The Atlantic Ocean Road features in the 2021 game 'Rims Racing.' In which country would you find that great ride?

SESSION 8: GENERAL (2)

Quiz 1: Anagrams – Manufacturers

Can you name the manufacturer from the anagram?

1. MWB.
2. DHAON.
3. UIUKZS.
4. HYAAAM.
5. AAKKISAW.
6. EAGRLI.
7. TCIAUD.
8. VRQUNAASRH.
9. LRPAAII.
10. PUTMIHR.

Quiz 2: True or False?

1. True or False: Leon Haslam is the nephew of the former road racer Ron Haslam?
2. True or False: Ducati is the sole manufacturer for the 2023 Moto-E World Championship?
3. True or False: KTM riders won the Dakar Rally for Bikes every year between 2001 and 2019?
4. True or False: Hero MotoCorp is a motorcycle manufacturer from China?
5. True or False: Ricky Carmichael won two races in NASCAR?
6. True or False: The first recorded Motocross competition was on Camberley Heath in Surrey, England on 29th March 1924?
7. True or False: The FIM Trial World Championship was known as Challenge Henry Groutards between 1964 and 1967?
8. True or False: In May 2015, the Philippine stuntman Gerard Jessie balanced a Honda step-thru motorcycle on his head for 31.2 seconds?
9. True or False: The North-West 200 features in the Ride 2 video game?
10. True or False: The slogan of Royal Enfield is "Built like a tank?"

Quiz 3: Circuits (1)

1. Which circuit, built in 1955, is popularly referred to as "The Cathedral" of motorcycling?
2. On which circuit would you find the Spoon Curve?
3. Can you name the Spanish racer who set a lap record of 1:20.554 at Laguna Seca during the 2012 United States Motorcycle Grand Prix?
4. Which circuit hosted the final round of the FIM Superbike World Championship in November 2008, just three weeks after it was opened?
5. In which country would you find the Cemetery Circuit?
6. At which circuit did Jock Taylor suffer a fatal accident in 1982?
7. What is the name of the circuit within the 24-hour circuit at Le Mans which hosts a round of MotoGP?
8. Which circuit was renamed on 3rd May 2018 in honour of the late Ángel Nieto?
9. Which of these German circuits hosted a motorcycle race first: Hockenheimring, Nürburgring, Sachsenring, or Oschersleben?
10. On which circuit would you find the Melbourne Corner?

Quiz 4: Circuits (2)

1. What is the Masaryk Circuit also known as?
2. In which country would you find the Automotodrom Grobnik?
3. Which circuit has corners called 'Maternity,' 'Police,' and 'Fishermen's?'
4. Who is the third corner at Phillip Island named after?
5. In 1993, vintage racing motorcyclist Chas Guy was killed in practice at the inaugural meeting of which annual motorsport event held in the UK?
6. Which circuit is in the town of Alcañiz in Spain?
7. Who is the Misano circuit named after?
8. Which circuit, opened in 1950, hosted a round of the FIM Superbike World Championship in 1993, then every year from 1995 to 2008?
9. True or False: In 2018, the Slovakia Ring hosted a round of the FIM Superbike World Championship?
10. Which circuit hosted the last round of the 2021 FIM Sidecar World Championship?

Quiz 5: Snaefell Mountain Course (1)

1. How long is one lap of the Snaefell Mountain Course?
2. On what road is the start/finish line located?
3. What name is given to the part of the course between the Bungalow and Brandywell on the mountain section?
4. At which milestone would you find Drinkwater's Bend?
5. The Raven pub is located next to which popular TT vantage point?
6. What is the name of the hill in Ramsey where Cruikshank's Corner and White Gates are located?
7. Whose cottage would you find on the right hander just after Glen Helen?
8. The location of a speed trap, where is the fastest part of the course?
9. What descriptive name is often given by riders to Ballagarey?
10. What is the name of the left-hander at the end of the Mountain Mile?

Quiz 6: Snaefell Mountain Course (2)

1. In 2017, a corner on the course was named after a non-competitor for the first time, who was it named after?
2. Which bend is sometimes referred to as "Milky's" after Richard 'Milky' Quayle crashed there during TT 2003?
3. Who resides next to the last series of corners on the course?
4. What is the name of the hill that rises out of Union Mills towards Glen Vine?
5. Who is the fast right-hander at the end of Cronk-y-Voddy straight named after?
6. Where on the course are the Conker Fields?
7. At which milestone is the corner known as 'Duke's', named after the late Geoff Duke?
8. Laurel Bank is in which section of the course?
9. In which village would you find The Railway Inn?
10. The 26th milestone is named after which TT legend?

Quiz 7: Who Am I?

Can you name the riders, past and present, from the cryptic clues?

1. I was born in Spain in February 1993. I won the MotoGP World Championship six times and am nicknamed the 'Ant of Cervera.'
2. I won five races in one day at the 1996 Ulster Grand Prix and own a motorcycle dealership in Lisburn, Northern Ireland, specialising in Triumph, Kawasaki, and KTM bikes.
3. In 2014, I became the first British rider to win a stage of the Dakar Rally since John Deacon in 1998, then followed that up by winning the race in 2017, something which I repeated in 2022.
4. I won the Superbike World Championship three times and a MotoGP race, all with Ducati. In 2009, I entered the Bathurst 1000 V8 Supercar race but when the rain came down on lap 77, I crashed at the Dipper and was forced to retire.
5. I was a nine-time Isle of Man TT sidecar winner who was left paralyzed in a crash in the 1993 Classic Manx Grand Prix. I died in March 2006 at the age of fifty-eight.
6. My two older brothers were successful motorcycle racers and I soon followed them, becoming the first-ever World Champion in my discipline in 1975. I helped my son achieve an incredible twelve World titles before I sadly passed away in April 2016, aged sixty-five.
7. Born in Murcia, Spain, in March 1997, I am the first woman in history to win a World Championship in solo motorcycle road racing.
8. A 1984 computer game carried my name. I worked as a stunt double for Timothy Dalton in the Living Daylights and Pierce Brosnan in GoldenEye. I was paralysed and suffered brain damage following an accident in 1996.

9. I was World Champion in 1993 and my racing number was retired as a mark of respect by FIM when I retired two years later. I co-designed the Circuit of the Americas racetrack with Tavo Hellmund and Hermann Tilke.
10. I set the lap record for a female rider at the Isle of Man TT in 2009, which I improved on in 2010. Later that year I won the first ever UK Electric Bike Racing (TTXgp) Championship.

Quiz 8: Miscellany (2)

1. Which Enduro star is featured on an Isle of Man fifty pence coin issued in 2012?
2. How many laps does a speedway race consist of?
3. On which circuit is the famous corkscrew turn?
4. Which MotoGP star is nicknamed, 'The Bakery?'
5. In which country would you find the Autódromo Termas de Rio Hondo?
6. Who won the MX2 Motocross World Championship in 2017?
7. On which circuit was Jimmy Guthrie tragically killed in 1937?
8. Can you name the two-time Endurance World Champion who ran the Diablo 666 Endurance Racing Team?
9. What do you call the mogul-like section of a motocross track which consists of ten or more tiny jumps in a row?
10. Who set a lap record with a time of 1:50.616 at the 2018 IRRC Imatranajo in Finland?

Quiz 9: Miscellany (3)

1. Which country hosted the first Motocross des Nations in 1947?
2. On which circuit did Dan Hegarty suffer a fatal accident in 2017?
3. What is the English translation of the Italian word 'Vespa?'
4. Which town in Spain has hosted a road race in August every year since 1954 to celebrate its festival of the Virgin Mary?
5. Why did some riders propose to boycott the 2011 MotoGP race at Motegi?
6. Who was Speedway World Champion in 2013, 2015, and 2018?
7. What was the nickname of Colin Edwards?
8. How many races did Davey Todd win at the 2023 North-West 200?
9. What term is given to dirt or debris thrown into the air from the force of a spinning rear tire whilst riding?
10. Which two musical instruments were the first products of Torakusu Yamaha and his company, Nippon Gakki Co. Ltd (now the Yamaha Corporation)?

Quiz 10: Anagrams – Riders

Can you name the rider from the anagram?

1. NEINLVAOT SISOR.
2. LECAIMH ONDPLU.
3. HEENATSP HEEENARTLPS.
4. LEVE EELNIVK.
5. RCLA RFYATGO.
6. ANYR OOIVOLTPL.
7. MAOIOCG ITOASING.
8. AXM GABIIG.
9. VEETS BTESWRE.
10. IFDEESRIG ZAUHCUS.

ANSWERS

SESSION 1: GENERAL (1)

Quiz 1: History of the Motorcycle

1. True (The Butler Petrol Cycle was the conception of Edward Butler in 1884); 2. Gottlieb Daimler and Wilhelm Maybach; 3. Michaux-Perreaux Steam Velocipede and the Roper Steam Velocipede; 4. Hildebrand and Wolfmüller Motorrad; 5. Peugeot Motorcycles; 6. 1901; 7. True; 8. Harley-Davidson; 9. BSA; 10. California.

Quiz 2: International Motorcycling Federation

1. 1904; 2. Switzerland; 3. Environmental Code; 4. True; 5. Jorge Viegas; 6. Seven; 7. False (it gained official status at the Sydney Olympics in 2000); 8. A wheel; 9. Giacomo Agostini; 10. 120 (116 to be precise).

Quiz 3: It's All About the Bike

1. False (they were added in 1928 by Harley Davidson); 2. Walter Kaaden; 3. Anti-lock Braking System; 4. Suzuki GT750; 5. Ethanol Flex Fuel; 6. BMW; 7. Honda CB750 Four; 8. 1960s; 9. True; 10. The vehicle disc brake.

Quiz 4: Manufacturers

1. True; 2. Suzuki; 3. Ten; 4. Spain; 5. Harley Davidson; 6. 1920s; 7. Lambretta motorscooter; 8. Indian; 9. Austria; 10. Royal Enfield.

Quiz 5: Motorcycling Legends

1. Valentino Rossi; 2. True; 3. Five; 4. Joey Dunlop; 5. 1976 500cc German Grand Prix; 6. Ángel Nieto; 6. John Surtees; 8. Ten; 9. Geoff Duke; 10. False (Stéphane Peterhansel holds the record with six wins).

Quiz 6: Motorcycling Records

1. Gene Walker; 2. Bonneville; 3. Patrick Fürstenhoff (aka Ghost Rider); 4. World's smallest motorcycle; 5. Eight; 6. True; 7. The Captain America Harley Davidson Panhead ridden by Peter Fonda in the 1969 film, Easy Rider; 8. Longest ride on water and fastest ride on water; 9. 60 (58 to be precise); 10. 26.

Quiz 7: Great Rides (1)

1. Arkansas; 2. Canada; 3. 50 (48 to be precise); 4. False (it's on the South Island); 5. Mexico; 6. Friendship Highway; 7. Douro; 8. Nashville, Tennessee; 9. Peak District; 10. South Africa.

Quiz 8: Great Rides (2)

1. California; 2. False (it's a hill in the south of the island); 3. The Great Ocean Road; 4. Pakistan and China; 5. Norway; 6. Alaska; 7. True; 8. Romania; 9. Icefields Parkway; 10. Peru.

Quiz 9: Miscellany (1)

1. A lap of the Snaefell Mountain Course on one wheel; 2. Chimay; 3. Cookbooks; 4. Twice; 5. The Flying Haggis; 6. Aberdare Park; 7. Minsk; 8. Che Guevara; 9. Denmark; 10. False (he raced for Red Bull KTM Factory Team).

Quiz 10: Anagrams – Circuits

1. Guai; 2. Dundrod; 3. Laguna Seca; 4. Billown; 5. Assen; 6. Mugello; 7. Paul Ricard; 8. Imatra; 9. Phillip Island; 10. Snaefell Mountain Course.

SESSION 2: TRACK RACING

Quiz 1: MotoGP (1)

1. 2002; 2. Thailand; 3. Bridgestone; 4. Qatar; 5. Carbon Disc Brakes; 6. Four; 7. Riding for a factory team unless said manufacturer lacked a satellite team; 8. Sepang (Malaysia); 9. KTM; 10. 430 (432 to be precise).

Quiz 2: MotoGP (2)

1. Neil Hodgson and Jeremy McWilliams; 2. Marco Melandri; 3. False (he's younger); 4. Dani Pedrosa; 5. Suzuki; 6. True; 7. 20; 8. Front ride-height (or holeshot) devices; 9. Kazakhstan and India; 10. 40 (18 fronts and 22 rears).

Quiz 3: MotoGP (3)

1. Scott Redding; 2. 250cc two stroke class; 3. Luis Salom; 4. Triumph; 5. Aprilia Racing Team Gresini; 6. Enea Bastianini; 7. Jorge Martin; 8. True; 9. Izan Guevara; 10. Pedro Acosta.

Quiz 4: GP World Championships {Pre-MotoGP} (1)

1. 1949; 2. Nations Grand Prix; 3. 15; 4. Argentina in 1961; 5. Riding a Manx Norton, he was the last to win a 500cc Grand Prix on a single-cylinder machine; 6. Phil Read; 7. Freddie Spencer and Kenny Roberts; 8. True; 9. Wayne Rainey; 10. Àlex Crivillé in 1999.

Quiz 5: GP World Championship {Pre-MotoGP} (2)

1. Gilera; 2. Tom Phillis; 3. True; 4. The financial costs of competing had spiralled out of control; 5. Derbi; 6. Finnish; 7. Kenny Roberts and Kenny Roberts Jr; 8. False (he won the 125cc title six times and the 250cc title three times); 9. 350cc; 10. Asia (the Japanese Grand Prix was first held in 1963, the United States Grand Prix was first held in 1964).

Quiz 6: World Superbikes (1)

1. 1988; 2. Four; 3. Colin Edwards; 4. Raymond Roche (in 1990); 5. Two; 6. Imola; 7. Chaz Davies; 8. Ten; 9. Álvaro Bautista; 10. Pirelli.

Quiz 7: World Superbikes (2)

1. True; 2. EuroSpeedway Lausitz and Magny-Cours; 3. Yamaha; 4. Cal Crutchlow; 5. Argentina; 6. Sylvain Guintoli and Eugene Laverty; 7. Three; 8. Isaac Viñales; 9. Turkish; 10. 25.

Quiz 8: Sidecar World Championship

1. Eric Oliver; 2. John Robinson; 3. Yamaha; 4. Seven; 5. Hub centre; 6. Steve Webster and Tony Hewitt; 7. Monkey; 8. Louis Christen; 9. Patrick Farrance; 10. True.

Quiz 9: British Superbikes (1)

1. Darren Dixon; 2. Twice; 3. Hodgkin Lymphoma; 4. Swan Yamaha; 5. Gregorio Lavilla; 6. MotorSport Vision; 7. False (he's won six titles); 8. Assen; 9. Glenn Irwin; 10. Eurosport and Quest.

Quiz 10: British Superbikes (2)

1. Cadwell Park; 2. Sean Emmett and Michael Rutter (both at Rockingham); 3. Snow; 4. The Privateers Cup; 5. Three; 6. Ryuichi Kiyonari; 7. Bimota; 8. Jake Dixon; 9. Any four from Donington Park National, Snetterton 300, Silverstone National, Oulton Park International, Donington Park GP, and Brands Hatch GP; 10. South African.

SESSION 3: ROAD RACING

Quiz 1: North-West 200 (1)

1. 1929; 2. The Triangle; 3. 9 miles (8.970mi to be precise); 4. Jack Brett; 5. Ballysally; 6. Bob McIntyre; 7. Coleraine and District Motor Club; 8. Three; 9. Tom Herron, Brian Hamilton, and Frank Kennedy; 10. True.

Quiz 2: North-West 200 (2)

1. David Jefferies; 2. Superstock (in 2008); 3. BMW; 4. Hoax bomb alert; 5. False (it was Martin Jessopp); 6. 15; 7. A significant increase in the insurance premium; 8. Church Corner; 9. FHO Racing; 10. Cory West.

Quiz 3: Ulster Grand Prix

1. 1922; 2. Old Clady Circuit; 3. Dundrod; 4. 7 miles (7.401mi to be precise); 5. Twice; 6. False (Gary Hocking won in 1961, Redman won the other years); 7. Ángel Nieto; 8. The political situation in Northern Ireland; 9. True; 10. 24.

Quiz 4: Macau Motorcycle Grand Prix

1. 1967; 2. Guia; 3. 4 miles (3.803mi to be precise); 4. Chas Mortimer; 5. Nine; 6. Ducati 1199RS; 7. False (he won the 2001 race); 8. Lisboa; 9. Robert; 10. Erno Kostamo.

Quiz 5: Manx Grand Prix (1)

1. 1923; 2. The Manx Motorcycle Club; 3. Bob Heath (with 11 wins); 4. Senior MGP; 5. True; 6. Gloria Clark; 7. Four; 8. Geoff Duke; 9. Tommy Clucas; 10. Robert Dunlop.

Quiz 6: Manx Grand Prix (2)

1. Cronk-ny-Mona; 2. 2010; 3. Poor weather conditions; 4. First female winner on the Snaefell Mountain Course; 5. Junior MGP; 6. Jamie Hodson; 7. Union Mills; 8. False (22 nations were represented); 9. Two; 10. Classic Superbike MGP.

Quiz 7: Classic TT (2013-2019)

1. Ollie Linsdell; 2. 1967 Senior TT; 3. The Italian National Anthem; 4. Norton; 5. Michael Rutter; 6. Vintage Motorcycle Club; 7. False (he set the record in 2017); 8. John McGuinness; 9. Steve Hislop; 10. Two.

Quiz 8: Southern 100 Road Races

1. Billown; 2. 1955; 3. Castletown; 4. St Lupus, Kirk Malew; 5. Ian Lougher; 6. Clerk of the Course; 7. 1962; 8. Dave Leach; 9. 350cc; 10. Michael Dunlop.

Quiz 9: Scarborough

1. Oliver's Mount; 2. 1946; 3. Farm Bends; 4. Guy Martin; 5. False (it's 2.43 miles long); 6. Dean Harrison; 7. Three; 8. True; 9. Barry Sheene; 10. Joey Thompson.

Quiz 10: Other Irish Road Races

1. Tandragee 100; 2. Supersport and Moto3/125cc; 3. Derek Shiels; 4. Kells; 5. Mervyn Robinson, Frank Kennedy, and

brothers Joey & Jim Dunlop; 6. 5 miles (5.3 miles to be precise); 7. 2018; 8. True; 9. Michael Sweeney; 10. Martin Finnegan.

SESSION 4: Isle of Man TT (1)

Quiz 1: Isle of Man TT - General (1)

1. Tourist Trophy; 2. St John's Short Course; 3. Charles Collier; 4. 1935; 5. Joey Dunlop (with 26); 6. 10 seconds; 7. Inge Stoll, 1954 Sidecar TT; 8. Clerk of the Course; 9. 17; 10. World Wars I & II, outbreak of Foot and Mouth disease in 2001, and the Covid-19 pandemic in 2020 & 2021.

Quiz 2: Isle of Man TT: 1907-1914

1. 25; 2. £25; 3. Jack Marshall; 4. Quarterbridge Road; 5. Percy Evans; 6. First 50mph lap on the Mountain Course; 7. They complained that the new mountain course was too arduous; 8. Frank R. Bateman; 9. The wearing of crash helmets; 10. Eric and Cyril Williams.

Quiz 3: Isle of Man TT: 1920s

1. 1923 Junior TT; 2. Tommy de la Hay; 3. Howard 'R' Davies; 4. First Manxman to win a TT race; 5. 14; 6. Freddie Dixon and T. W. Denny; 7. A puncture; 8. Second; 9. Alec Bennett; 10. Greeba Bridge.

Quiz 4: Isle of Man TT: 1930s

1. Valve problems; 2. BBC; 3. Percy "Tim" Hunt; 4. HRH Prince George; 5. False (Jimmie Guthrie won in 1934); 6. 1936 Junior TT; 7. First foreigner to win an Isle of Man TT race; 8. Six; 9. Ewald Kluge; 10. Ballaugh Bridge.

Quiz 5: Isle of Man TT: 1947-1959 (1)

1. Due to the low quality "pool" petrol available and the ban on superchargers; 2. Harold Daniell; 3. 100; 4. Ballig Bridge; 5. Geoff Duke; 6. Ben Drinkwater; 7. 0.2 seconds; 8. Artie Bell; 9. Ultra-Lightweight TT; 10. 1949.

Quiz 6: Isle of Man TT: 1947-1959 (2)

1. True; 2. Ray Amm; 3. Sidecar TT; 4. Clubman's Junior TT; 5. Bill Lomas; 6. Six; 7. Lightweight and Ultra-Lightweight TT; 8. Bob McIntyre; 9. False (he won three); 10. 1952 Ultra-Lightweight TT.

Quiz 7: Isle of Man TT: 1960s (1)

1. 1964; 2. Gary Hocking; 3. Helmut Fath; 4. Senior TT, Lightweight 250cc TT, and Lightweight 125cc TT; 5. Eight; 6. Laurel Bank; 7. Suzuki; 8. Luigi Taveri; 9. Mitsuo Itoh (who won the 50cc race); 10. 1960 Senior TT.

Quiz 8: Isle of Man TT: 1960s (2)

1. Jim Redman; 2. He had a virus which kept him in bed for four days; 3. Sarah's Cottage; 4. A seamen's strike; 5. False (Chris Vincent piloted a BSA to victory in the 1962 race); 6. John Hartle; 7. A broken chain; 8. Bill Ivy; 9. Barry Smith; 10. Kawasaki.

Quiz 9: Isle of Man TT: 1970s (1)

1. 1974 Production 1000cc TT; 2. Kel Carruthers; 3. Klaus Enders and Wolfgang Kalauch; 4. Barry Sheene; 5. Tony Jefferies; 6. Gilberto Parlotti; 7. Jack Findlay; 8. Nine; 9. 1973 Lightweight 125cc TT; 10. Chas Mortimer.

Quiz 10: Isle of Man TT: 1970s (2)

1. Ten; 2. Charlie Williams; 3. His chain came off his Yamaha as he jumped Ballaugh Bridge; 4. Two; 5. Bill Simpson and Chas Mortimer; 6. Jubilee TT; 7. Alan Jackson; 8. Pat Hennen; 9. Trevor Ireson and Clive Pollington; 10. 1978 Formula One and 1979 Senior TT.

SESSION 5: Isle of Man TT (2)

Quiz 1: Isle of Man TT: 1980s (1)

1. Graeme Crosby; 2. Jock Taylor and Benga Johansson; 3. 1985; 4. Ron Haslam; 5. Second; 6. 1985 Production 750cc TT; 7. Mick Boddice; 8. Dave Roper, who won the 500cc class in the Historic TT; 9. Greeba Bridge; 10. 1987 Formula Two.

Quiz 2: Isle of Man TT: 1980s (2)

1. Four; 2. Silver Dream Racer; 3. Gene McDonnell; 4. 32nd Milestone; 5. 1989 750cc Production TT; 6. False (it was Barry Woodland); 7. Steve Cull; 8. Steve Hislop; 9. Doran's Bend; 10. Dave Molyneux.

Quiz 3: Isle of Man TT: 1990s (1)

1. 1992 Ultra-Lightweight TT; 2. Ian Lougher; 3. Carl Fogarty; 4. Dave Savile; 5. Geoff Bell and Keith Cornbill; 6. 31; 7. Britten V1000; 8. Jim Moodie; 9. Robert Dunlop; 10. Brandywell.

Quiz 4: Isle of Man TT: 1990s (2)

1. Two; 2. Rob Fisher and Michael Wynn; 3. Mark Baldwin; 4. Formula One TT, Junior TT, Production TT, and Senior TT; 5. Dave Morris; 6. True; 7. The starting order was decided by the overall practice leader board; 8. Joey Dunlop; 9. Bob Jackson; 10. Paul Orritt.

Quiz 5: Isle of Man TT: 2000s (1)

1. Formula One TT, Lightweight 250cc TT, and Ultra Lightweight TT; 2. Estonia; 3. Lightweight 400cc TT; 4. Giacomo Agostini; 5. Triumph; 6. Chris Palmer (Honda); 7. Shaun Harris; 8. Nine; 9. 2004 Production 600cc TT; 10. Ian 'Gus' Scott.

Quiz 6: Isle of Man TT: 2000s (2)

1. TT 2007; 2. Nick Crowe and Darren Hope; 3. 2007 Supersport TT; 4. Cameron Donald; 5. Waterworks Corner; 6. Honda; 7. Rob Barber; 8. 2009 Supersport TT; 9. Steve Plater; 10. Eight (four with Dave Molyneux, three with Klaus Klaffenbock, and one with Tim Reeves).

Quiz 7: Isle of Man TT: 2010s (1)

1. 2013; 2. Five; 3. Conor Cummins; 4. Mark Miller; 5. Gary Johnson; 6. Poor weather conditions; 7. Ryan Farquhar; 8. Twelve; 9. James May; 10. Michael Dunlop.

Quiz 8: Isle of Man TT: 2010s (2)

1. Bray Hill; 2. Conrad and Dean Harrison; 3. Mugen; 4. Mark Higgins; 5. Keith Flint (the late singer of the Prodigy); 6. Ivan Lintin; 7. Suter MMX500 V4 2 Stroke; 8. Superbike TT and Superstock TT; 9. Steve Mercer; 10. Superstock TT, Supersport Two TT, Lightweight TT, TT Zero and Sidecar Race Two.

Quiz 9: Isle of Man TT: 2022

1. Two; 2. Amy Williams; 3. Sam West and Dave Moffitt; 4. Tyre failure; 5. False (it took him to 21 wins); 6. Paul Jordan; 7. Third; 8. Michael Russell; 9. Dean Harrison; 10. Faye Ho.

Quiz 10: Isle of Man TT - General (2)

1. Ramsey; 2. Victor Surridge (in 1911); 3. May; 4. The Lady in White; 5. Joey Dunlop Foundation; 6. 33; 7. Bushy's; 8. Maurice Mawdsley; 9. 2004; 10. Onchan (near Port Jack).

SESSION 6: DISCIPLINES AND EVENTS

Quiz 1: Enduro (1)

1. True; 2. Three; 3. New Zealand; 4. Grand National Cross-Country Series; 5. Canada; 6. True; 7. Sherco; 8. Austria; 9. Billy Bolt; 10. Up to 250cc two stroke and four stroke.

Quiz 2: Enduro (2)

1. False (it was Steve McQueen); 2. Czech; 3. Tadeusz Błażusíak; 4. Eight; 5. Husaberg; 6. For not completing the required course; 7. Eero Remes; 8. Italy; 9. Manuel Lettenbichler; 10. Portugal.

Quiz 3: Motocross

1. Scrambles Racing; 2. Holland; 3. Suzuki; 4. Akira Watanabe; 5. First person to win a major motocross title on a four-stroke powered machine; 6. 30 minutes plus two laps; 7. Tony Cairoli; 8. Twice; 9. Puerto Rico; 10. Nancy van de Ven.

Quiz 4: Speedway

1. Australia; 2. Star Riders' Championship; 3. Wembley; 4. 425 metres; 5. Methanol with no additives; 6. Four; 7. Robert Lambert; 8. Poland; 9. Egon Müller (in 1983); 10. Belle Vue Aces.

Quiz 5: Trials

1. Scott Trial; 2. One point; 3. Fort William; 4. Poland; 5. Seven; 6. Sam Cooper; 7. Takahisa Fujinami; 8. Five; 9. True; 10. James Dabill.

Quiz 6: Electric Bikes

1. Indian Motorcycle Company; 2. True; 3. Twice; 4. Peugeot (Scoot 'Elec); 5. A fire at the Jerez test in March where all competition bikes were destroyed; 6. Matteo Ferrari; 7. Circuit Bugatti, Le Mans; 8. Dominique Aegerter; 9. Energica; 10. False (it's 270km/h).

Quiz 7: Supermoto

1. Carlsbad Raceway; 2. 2003; 3. Gilera (Nordwest model); 4. Thierry Van Den Bosch; 5. Eight; 6. Jeff Ward; 7. Dunlop; 8. 2009; 9. Aprilia; 10. Mark-Reiner Schmidt.

Quiz 8: Endurance World Championship

1. Six hours; 2. False (the circuit was at Vaujours near Paris); 3. Thruxton; 4. Brian Morrison; 5. Three; 6. Suzuki GSX-R 1000; 7. David Checa; 8. Suzuka in Japan and Sepang in Malaysia; 9. BMW; 10. Yoshimura SERT Motul.

Quiz 9: Dakar Rally

1. 1979; 2. Thierry Sabine; 3. GPS; 4. Gilles Lalay; 5. Granada; 6. Five; 7. Fears of attacks in Mauritania following the killing of four French tourists a few weeks before; 8. Matthias Walkner; 9. Peru; 10. James Hillier.

Quiz 10: Pikes Peak International Hill Climb

1. 1916; 2. Race to the Clouds; 3. False (they won twice in 1954 and 1955) 4. 12 miles (12.42 to be precise); 5. Bobby Parr; 6. 160 (156 to be precise); 7. True (about 25% of the course was dirt); 8. Bruno Langlois (in 2016); 9. Carlin Dunne; 10. 2018 Aprilia Tuono V4 1100.

SESSION 7: ENTERTAINMENT

Quiz 1: At the Movies (1)

1. Michelle Pfeiffer; 2. False (it was filmed in 2010); 3. Billy; 4. Terminator 2: Judgment Day; 5. Burt Munro; 6. Stone; 7. Marlon Brando; 8. The Girl on a Motorcycle; 9. John Travolta and Martin Lawrence; 10. The Dark Knight.

Quiz 2: At the Movies (2)

1. Triumph TT Special 650; 2. Gene Kelly; 3. The Wild Angels; 4. The Motorcycle Diaries; 5. Wes Anderson; 6. Tron: Legacy; 7. Brad Pitt; 8. The races at Daytona; 9. Peter Fonda; 10. The Dunlops.

Quiz 3: Celebrity Bikers

1. Ryan Reynolds; 2. Orlando Bloom; 3. True; 4. P!nk; 5. Yamaha; 6. Keanu Reeves; 7. You Oughta Know; 8. Mr T; 9. James Dean; 10. Tom Hardy.

Quiz 4: Literature

1. Sirius Black; 2. Cephalonia; 3. Ted Hughes; 4. Isle of Man TT; 5. Hunter S. Thompson; 6. John Hopkins; 7. Mouse; 8. Charley Boorman; 9. Harley Davidson; 10. Ride a motorcycle around the World.

Quiz 5: Music (1)

1. Emptiness; 2. Easy Rider; 3. Hopscotch; 4. Jasper Carrot; 5. Mexico; 6. Nowhere; 7. Nelly; 8. Bat Out of Hell; 9. Saxon; 10. A steel horse.

Quiz 6: Music (2)

1. Arlo Guthrie; 2. Hell; 3. Willie Nelson; 4. Dumpy's Rusty Nuts; 5. The Head Nurse; 6. Joe Satriani; 7. Jimmy; 8. Isle of Man TT; 9. Sons of Anarchy; 10. The Beach Boys.

Quiz 7: Television (1)

1. BMW; 2. Street Hawk; 3. David Beckham; 4. The Hairy Bikers; 5. True; 6. The Walking Dead; 7. Discovery Channel; 8. Harley and the Davidsons; 9. Michael Elphick; 10. False (its about the Isle of Man TT).

Quiz 8: Television (2)

1. Kick Start; 2. True; 3. Paul Teutul Sr. and Paul Teutul Jr; 4. Pike's Peak International Hill Climb; 5. False (though George Clooney did!); 6. Harley Davidson LiveWire electric motorcycles; 7. Two Fat Ladies; 8. Heartbeat; 9. Henry Cole; 10. 1996.

Quiz 9: Video Games (1)

1. Action Biker and Road Rash; 2. Hang On; 3. Mars; 4. Jeremy McGrath; 5. Jester Interactive; 6. Shadow the Hedgehog; 7. Gran Turismo; 8. Ride to Hell: Retribution; 9. LocoCycle; 10. Saber Interactive.

Quiz 10: Video Games (2)

1. 22nd; 2. Nacon (formerly BigBen Interactive); 3. Final Fantasy (it first appears in Final Fantasy 7); 4. PlayStation; 5. Polecats; 6. Milestone SRL; 7. Four; 8. Ubisoft; 9. Devil May Cry 5; 10. Norway.

SESSION 8: GENERAL (2)

Quiz 1: Anagrams – Manufacturers

1. BMW; 2. Honda; 3. Suzuki; 4. Yamaha; 5. Kawasaki; 6. Gilera; 7. Ducati; 8. Husqvarna; 9. Aprilia; 10. Triumph.

Quiz 2: True or False?

1. False (he is his son!); 2. True; 3. True; 4. False (it is from India); 5. False (he didn't win any!); 6. True; 7. True; 8. False (he did balance one on his head but for a still remarkable 14.93 seconds not 31.2!); 9. True; 10. False (its "Built like a gun").

Quiz 3: Circuits (1)

1. Assen; 2. Suzuka; 3. Jorge Lorenzo; 4. Algarve International Circuit; 5. New Zealand; 6. Imatra in Finland; 7. Bugatti Circuit; 8. Jerez; 9. Sachsenring (in May 1927 just three weeks before the Nürburgring); 10. Donington Park.

Quiz 4: Circuits (2)

1. Brno Circuit; 2. Croatia; 3. Macau; 4. Casey Stoner; 5. Goodwood Festival of Speed; 6. MotorLand Aragon; 7. Marco Simoncelli; 8. Brands Hatch; 9. False (it hosted a round of the FIM Sidecar World Championship); 10. Estoril.

Quiz 5: Snaefell Mountain Course (1)

1. 37.73miles (60.725km); 2. Glencrutchery Road; 3. Hailwood's Rise; 4. 11th; 5. Ballaugh Bridge; 6. May Hill; 7. Sarah's; 8. Sulby Straight; 9. Ballascary; 10. Mountain Box, or East Mountain Gate.

Quiz 6: Snaefell Mountain Course (2)

1. Raymond Caley, a Sulby shopkeeper and TT marshall, who had died earlier that year; 2. Ballaspur; 3. The Lieutenant Governor; 4. Ballahutchin; 5. Dave Molyneux; 6. Churchtown; 7. 32nd; 8. Glen Helen; 9. Union Mills; 10. Joey Dunlop.

Quiz 7: Who Am I?

1. Marc Márquez; 2. Phillip McCallen; 3. Sam Sunderland; 4. Troy Bayliss; 5. Dave Saville; 6. Harold Martin Lampkin; 7. Ana Carrasco; 8. Eddie Kidd; 9. Kevin Schwantz; 10. Jenny Tinmouth.

Quiz 8: Miscellany (2)

1. David Knight; 2. Four; 3. Laguna Seca; 4. Álex Rins; 5. Argentina; 6. Pauls Jonass; 7. Sachsenring; 8. Terry Rymer; 9. Whoops; 10. Danny Webb.

Quiz 9: Miscellany (3)

1. Netherlands; 2. Macau; 3. Wasp; 4. La Bañeza; 5. Radiation from the Fukushima Daiichi Nuclear Power Plant prompted health fears amongst riders and teams; 6. Tai Woffinden; 7. Texas Tornado; 8. Two; 9. Roost; 10. Reed Organs and Pianos.

Quiz 10: Anagrams – Riders

1. Valentino Rossi; 2. Michael Dunlop; 3. Stéphane Peterhansel; 4. Evel Knievel; 5. Carl Fogarty; 6. Ryan Villopoto; 7. Giacomo Agostini; 8. Max Biaggi; 9. Steve Webster; 10. Siegfried Schauzu.

ABOUT THE AUTHOR

Philip Carter is a cycling enthusiast and has travelled all over the World to watch bike races. As a proud Manxman he was privileged to be in France in 2011 and 2016 to see Mark Cavendish wearing the Green and Yellow Jerseys. He counts the Tour Down Under as the best stage race, for accessibility to the riders and stages, the weather and of course the wine. He has ridden cyclosportives in Flanders and the UK and cycled up the odd Pyrenean mountain. Aside from cycling, Manchester United is his other passion and he tries to attend a couple of matches each season.

BOOKS BY THE AUTHOR

- The Ultimate Cycling Quiz Book: 800 questions about cycling and there's even a music round!
- The Ultimate Farming Quiz Book: 600 questions about agriculture
- The Ultimate Isle of Man Quiz Book: 850 questions about Manx Life, including the World-Famous Motorcycle Races.
- The Ultimate Manchester United Quiz Book: 800 questions about the Red Devils.
- The Ultimate Spain Quiz Book: 500 questions about Spanish life.
- The Ultimate World Soccer Quiz Book: 1800 questions about the beautiful game.
- Cycling in the Isle of Man: A nine stage 'Tour de Mann' through the homeland of the Manx Missile.
- Historic Tour De France: A Cycling Novelette.

ALL BOOKS AVAILABLE ON AMAZON.

Printed in Dunstable, United Kingdom